COVENANT • BIBLE • STUDIES

Sermon on the Mount

Robert C. Bowman

faithQuest ◆ Brethren Press

Unless otherwise noted, scripture quotations are from the Revised Standard Version of the Bible, copyrighted 1946, 1952, 1971, 1973, 1977 by the National Council of Churches of Christ in the USA, Division of Education and Ministry.

Cover design by Kathy Kline Miller

97   96   95   94   93   5   4   3   2

International Standard Book Number: 0-87178-777-6

Library of Congress Cataloging-in-Publication Data

Bowman, Robert C., 1934 -
    Sermon on the mount / Robert C. Bowman.
        p. cm. — (Covenant Bible study series)
    Bibliography: p.
    ISBN 0-87178-777-6
    1. Sermon on the mount—Textbooks. I. Title. II. Series.
BT380.2.B69 1988
226'.9'0076—dc19   88-22328

Manufactured in the United States of America

Contents

Foreword

The Covenant Bible Study Series was first developed for a denominational program in the Church of the Brethren and the Christian Church (Disciples of Christ). This program, called People of the Covenant, was founded on the concept of relational Bible study and has been adopted by several other denominations and small groups who want to study the Bible in a community rather than alone.

Relational Bible study is marked by certain characteristics, some of which differ from other types of Bible study. For one, it is intended for small groups of people who can meet face-to-face on a regular basis and share frankly with an intimate group.

It is important to remember that relational Bible study is anchored in covenantal history. God covenanted with people in Old Testament history, established a new covenant in Jesus Christ, and covenants with the church today.

Relational Bible study takes seriously a corporate faith. As each person contributes to study, prayer, and work, the group becomes the real body of Christ. Each one's contribution is needed and important. "For just as the body is one and has many members, and all the members of the body, though many, are one body, so it is with Christ. . . . Now you are the body of Christ and individually members of it" (1 Cor. 12:12, 17).

Relational Bible study helps both individuals and the group to claim the promise of the Spirit and the working of the Spirit. As one person testified, "In our commitment to one another and in our sharing, something happened. . . . We were woven together in love by the master Weaver. It is something that can happen only when two or three or seven are gathered in God's name and we know the promise of God's presence in our lives."

The symbol for these covenant Bible study groups is the burlap cross. The interwoven threads, the uniqueness of each strand, the unrefined fabric, and the rough texture characterize covenant groups. The people in the groups are unique but interrelated; they are imperfect and unpolished, but loving and supportive.

The shape that these divergent threads create is the cross, the symbol for all Christians of the resurrection and presence with us of Christ our Savior. Like the burlap cross, we are brought together, simple and ordinary, to be sent out again in all directions to be in the world.

For people who choose to use this study in a small group, the following guidelines will help create an atmosphere in which support will grow and faith will deepen.

1. As a small group of learners, we gather around God's word to discern its meaning for today.
2. The words, stories, and admonitions we find in scripture come alive for today, challenging and renewing us.
3. All people are learners and all are leaders.
4. Each person will contribute to the study, sharing the meaning found in the scripture and helping to bring meaning to others.
5. We recognize each other's vulnerability as we share out of our own experience, and in sharing we learn to trust others and to be trustworthy.

Additional suggestions for study and group-building are provided in the "Sharing and Prayer" section. They are intended for use in the hour preceding the Bible study to foster intimacy in the covenant group and relate personal sharing to the Bible study topic.

Welcome to this study. As you search the scriptures, may you also search yourself. May God's voice and guidance and the love and encouragement of brothers and sisters in Christ challenge you to live more fully the abundant life God promises.

1

Keynote of a New Age
Matthew 4:17—5:1

Preparation

Read the suggested scripture for this session. It will also be helpful to read through the Sermon on the Mount (Matt. 5:2—7:27) at least once each week during this study.

Understanding

My first Bible was given to me at the age of eight. It was bound in black genuine leather and the edges of the pages were gold. It was a King James version with the words of Jesus in red. It looked, smelled, and felt holy. I was deeply impressed.

The Bible came about the time I first began to think about my religious life. I was strangely moved by the sermons of our guest evangelist. I asked my parents about baptism. An awakening was taking place inside of me. So when the Bible arrived, I wanted to "consecrate it" with some special act of devotion. As that act of devotion I chose to read through the Sermon on the Mount, a fairly major accomplishment for an eight-year old.

Later in life I asked myself, why did I choose the Sermon on the Mount? Why not Genesis, 1 Corinthians 13, the 23rd Psalm, or Galatians? What instinct prompted me to focus on the Sermon on the Mount as the appropriate place to begin my life in Christ?

Maybe the question isn't really "Why the Sermon on the Mount?" It probably is, "Why doesn't everybody choose the Sermon on the Mount?" Many Christians generally tend to view the Sermon on the Mount as the very heart of the faith. We agree with St. Augustine who called it "a perfect standard of the Christian life." More sermons are preached on the Sermon on the Mount in the Anabaptist and Pietist traditions than perhaps any other scripture.

Regardless of one's religious heritage, there is wisdom in the counsel, "Read the Old Testament in the light of the New Testament. Read the New Testament with the mind of Christ. And the mind of Christ is most fully revealed in the Sermon on the Mount."

So the Sermon on the Mount has been for many of us the touchstone by which all of scripture, and even all of our faith, was tested. Years later I discovered that some Christians chose other scripture passages as their "touchstone." But for many denominations, the Sermon on the Mount is the classic statement of one aspect of the Christian tradition. It also seemed appropriate to Matthew to give it a premier billing in his Gospel as the "keynote address" of Jesus.

Turning to Matthew's Gospel, let us examine the setting for the Sermon on the Mount. At the beginning of the ministry of Jesus, after his baptism and the temptation, Matthew inserts only three short summary statements before launching directly into the Sermon on the Mount.

The three statements are (1) an Old Testament text validating the location of Jesus' preaching with a one-line summary of that preaching; (2) the story of the calling of four of his twelve disciples—probably to be understood as typical of the way Jesus called all his disciples; and (3) a general statement about the public response to the healing and preaching ministry of Jesus.

These summary statements set the stage for the Sermon on the Mount. The statement about the healing and the public ministry of Jesus (Matt. 4:23–25) tells us two things. It tells us that Jesus has power and authority to heal, relieve pain, bring sanity, and restore wholeness. Second, it tells us that this is a major focus of his ministry. One can expect, therefore, that the Sermon on the Mount will be in harmony with this focus. One can expect that the purpose of the Sermon on the Mount is also for blessing, healing, and sanity.

The story of the calling of the disciples tells us that there is more to the story of Jesus than healing and blessing. The call to accept God's love is also the call to obey God's will and to join God's people. To put it another way, healing is not only a matter of having something done to you, it is also a matter of doing certain things or living certain ways. These two cannot be separated; salvation cannot be separated from a way of living. Jesus bids us to follow a way of life which he announces, a way which he describes, and a way which he is.

Finally, the summary sentence of Jesus' preaching is a key to the whole. "Repent. Heaven's reign is near." Matthew regularly says "kingdom of heaven" while Mark and Luke say "kingdom of

God." They mean precisely the same thing. Whether we translate it the kingdom of God or the reign of heaven or God's rule, this phrase represents a central part of the teaching and preaching of Jesus. It is, as one author says, "impossible to read the first three gospels with eyes open and not run up against the 'reign of God' every few lines." When we begin to uncork what Jesus meant by the phrase "kingdom of heaven," we come close to understanding the whole meaning of the life and work of Jesus.

The message of salvation, the ethical teaching, the forgiveness of sinners, the challenge to radical discipleship, the welcoming of the outcast, in fact, all of the themes of the New Testament, need to be understood in the context of the kingdom of God or they are misunderstood.

The concept of the kingdom of God is more complex than we will be able to deal with in one meeting. However, three aspects of it are important for a beginning. The first has to do with the translation of the word *kingdom*. When we think of *kingdom*, we normally think of a territory. A more accurate translation is to think of the power, or the authority, or the dignity, or the reigning of God. Perhaps the "kingship of God" is a better translation. In any event, the focus is on God, and especially upon God's beginning to assume the authority, the power, the centrality in the affairs of life and, most especially, within the network of human relationships. It is a way of taking God with utmost seriousness. It is saying that the world is no longer adrift. God has a purpose for human relationships and is beginning to work that purpose out.

A second aspect of the kingdom of God is the strange way the New Testament sends a double message. In some passages we are encouraged to look forward to the end of history when the kingdom of God will come. Some Christians stop with this meaning. They believe that war, economic oppression, racial discrimination, and social injustice will simply be with us "until kingdom come," as long as we have this world. But the New Testament has other passages in which we are encouraged to see that in some sense the kingdom of God has already come. Already there are places in the world in which that dignity, power, and reigning of God can be seen and experienced. The clearest and most powerful of these places is in Jesus. "The kingdom of God is among you."

The third aspect of the kingdom that is helpful for our understanding is that the church exists as a model of the kingdom. It is an outpost of the kingdom. The church is intended to be the place where one can see with special clarity the kind of human relationships which portray the reign of God. A church has a blessing and healing ministry, a special commitment to following Jesus, and a way of existing which draws attention to the dignity, authority, and rights of God.

Matthew sets the stage for this special sermon. A new reader of Matthew would come to chapter 5 with great expectations. We see Jesus, that very clear revelation of God, whose message is God's kingship, whose call is to follow, whose purpose is to heal and bless. Now, when he takes his seat on the mountain and begins to speak, we want to listen. We are convinced that what he will say will be the most important statement of what life is all about that we will ever hear.

Discussion and Action

For Beginning

Share stories about your own awakening interest in the Bible. What part of the Bible first had special meaning for you? Why?

For Discussion

1. What does it mean to pray, "Thy kingdom come"? In a good Bible dictionary or wordbook, look up the meaning of "kingdom of God" or "kingdom of heaven."

2. The author suggests that not all Christians look on the Sermon on the Mount as the most important scripture. What other passages might you suggest?

3. Does the Sermon on the Mount seem healing or disturbing? List the parts that are most disturbing to the group and the parts that seem the most healing.

2

Transformation or Despair
Matthew 5

Preparation

Linus, in the *Peanuts* cartoons, once was crushed by a B on his report card. He said, "There is no greater burden than having 'high potential.' " Recall occasions when someone had high expectations of you. Was it freeing or burdensome?

Understanding

The General Secretary of the Church of the Brethren tells of the day his daughter was diagnosed as having a rare fatal illness. Fortunately, it was discovered in time. Unfortunately, the only medicine available would probably leave her blind. The decision Don Miller and his wife, Phyllis, had to make was agonizing. If they gave their daughter the medicine, she would likely be permanently blinded. If they did not give her the medicine, she would most likely die.

After a heavy season of prayer, they decided to authorize the use of the medicine. A miracle occurred. By the grace of God their daughter was cured of the illness and retained her sight.

The Sermon on the Mount is strong medicine for the fatal ills of the world. It can lead persons to transformation and into the kingdom. However, there are occasions when the Sermon on the Mount has proven too overwhelming. It has led to despair.

Eberhard Arnold wrote about the Sermon on the Mount:

If we really grasp the Sermon on the Mount fully, if we really believe it, nothing can frighten us, neither our own self-recognition nor financial threats nor the weakness of the community, the weakness of its composition. Then we will be adequate to the situation, just as we are, in the midst of our weakness.

When we were beginning to go this way, the Sermon on the Mount shook us so powerfully that I simply cannot describe it. It spoke to me and encouraged me with tremendous force and depth. To me the most vital content of the Sermon on the Mount is the essence of salt, the warming blaze of light, the nature of the city community [the church], the life-power of the tree.

Unfortunately, not everyone feels this positive about the Sermon on the Mount. For some, the struggle to live up to its teachings is a source of frustration, alienation, and despair. They end up saying that although they admire the Sermon on the Mount, it cannot be related to contemporary life.

The story of theologian Friedrich Naumann is typical of many. Naumann began as an idealist, trying to live up to the demands of the Sermon on the Mount. Eventually he came to believe that the Sermon on the Mount cannot be fulfilled within the order of our civilization and, therefore, he concluded that it is no longer authoritative for us.

In 1903 Naumann said, "In this world Christianity has basically only two possibilities. Either it says: the disciple of Jesus can have nothing to do with the creating and acquiring activities of this age but must become a monk, or else it says that the disciple of Jesus Christ must recognize the limits of his Christianity. He must say, 'I will be Christian insofar as that is feasible in this world.' He must abandon the effort to live exclusively from Christian motives."

Naumann ended up a strong supporter of the German National Socialist Party and a staunch advocate of power politics during World War I. The Sermon on the Mount, rather than leading to transformation, in his case, led to despair. Strangely enough, he claimed to be a strong conservative Christian throughout this pilgrimage.

Naumann's story is extreme. Not so extreme are the hundreds of stories of persons who start their faith with full intention to surrender their will to the will of God, but who end up consumed by guilt, threatened with despair, and soured by a cynicism about the practicality of the Christian faith.

The Sermon on the Mount seems too strict, too high, too impossible for real life. One attractive solution is to turn from the Sermon on the Mount to the Apostle Paul. While the Sermon on the Mount seems to promote a religion of works, of human achievement, Paul comes to our rescue as the implacable foe of any suggestion that we can establish our own relationship with God by our own strength or activity. Some people say that the purpose of the

Sermon on the Mount is just to show us how right Paul is, that we need to be saved by faith and not works.

Robert Frost said, "The Sermon on the Mount is just a frame-up to insure the failure of all of us, so all of us will be thrown prostrate at the mercy seat for mercy." He called it the "irresistible beauty no one can live up to." Along with a host of interpreters of the Sermon on the Mount, he believes the purpose of the Sermon is to create despair so that we recognize how impossible it is to live up to God's demands, how sinful we are despite our best efforts, and how necessary it is that we cast ourselves on the grace of God. Theologian Gerhard Kittel said, "In the long run it [the Sermon on the Mount] has only one purpose: to expose and exhibit the great poverty in . . . human beings."

Of course, if one believes that the demands of the Sermon on the Mount are just a hoax to make us despair, then it is clear we don't have to take them seriously. One ends up taking the words of Jesus lightly so that one can follow Paul instead!

On the other hand, if one does choose to take the Sermon on the Mount seriously, then one must face the radical demands in it and our failure to live up to them. And then it is necessary to take with equal intensity Jesus and Paul.

How does one deal with the Sermon on the Mount and its impossibly high demands? Does it remain an irresistible beauty no one can live up to? Is it a source of guilt or of power? Is the Sermon on the Mount impossible?

Certainly the ideals of the Sermon on the Mount are high. But one must remember that Jesus was very realistic about human nature. Look at the assessment of Jesus about what is within us (Mark 7:20–23) or his treatment of the woman convicted of adultery (John 8:1–11). Jesus was no dreamy-eyed idealist about human nature. He knew us most profoundly and his program for action was always practical, do-able, and never made excessive demands on persons of good will who seek for God. He knew what was possible to us.

The Sermon on the Mount aims high, but to aim for the highest in life is one of the most human traits about us. Jason Martin declares that the longer one studies the Sermon on the Mount the more one concludes that it alone is possible. It is everything else in the world which is impossible, which doesn't work.

In the last session we discovered that the setting for the Sermon on the Mount included a summary of Jesus' ministry of healing, making whole, and bringing sanity. Therefore, as impossible as the demands of the Sermon on the Mount seem, as strange as its values appear, we are convinced that the message of the Sermon is not to drive us to despair, but to bring health and sanity.

Discussion and Action

For Beginning

What makes the difference between high expectations that are oppressive and those that are stimulating? What happens when one fails to meet the high expectations?

For Discussion

1. Where is the Sermon on the Mount a source of guilt for you? Where is it a source of power?

2. List examples from life today of situations where, for you, (a) the church is too legalistic and demands too much and (b) the church does not present God's demands in their severity.

3

Blessed Are the Wimps
Matthew 5:3-12

Preparation

Write a paraphrase of the eight Beatitudes. Perhaps it would be helpful to think of one or more persons who demonstrate the eight qualities listed here.

Understanding

Understanding the Beatitudes is not as easy as it first appears. In nearly every one there is a key word which is either hard to translate or is capable of several meanings. This seems to have been part of the teaching technique of Jesus. It may be that Jesus deliberately put his sayings into a form which demanded that the hearer make some personal investment. And the way we interpret his words becomes an exercise in spiritual maturity. No matter what size our jug, we get it filled at that fountain.

Another difficulty is the word *blessed.* Blessed is a word nobody uses outside of church. But what other word can we use? Happy is a bit weak to carry the meaning of blessed. Fortunate makes it all seem a matter of luck. For lack of something better, we will stick with blessed. As an additional exercise, you may want to make a list of synonyms for blessed: deep satisfaction, a special place in God's heart, becoming a true person, discovering the true meaning of joy, or knowing that at the deepest level things are all right.

Blessed are the poor in spirit, for theirs is the kingdom of heaven. The Beatitudes begin with one which is the most difficult to understand. Bluntly, the difficulty is that it is not clear whether Jesus is talking about money or attitude, economics or spirituality. Or both. Many translators and commentators believe Jesus was talking about some "spiritual" quality. *The Living Bible* changes this to "Humble men are very fortunate."

However, in a similar passage in Luke, the meaning of this passage is very clear, "Blessed are you poor" (Luke 6:20). Jesus is talking about real poor people. This has led other commentators to glamorize poverty romantically. But what makes poor people blessed is not the fact that they have no money. There's not much blessing in that. Yet poor people, in their seemingly endless experience of social and economic misery, discover that realities of the spirit can be learned in those circumstances which are hidden in others.

The phrase "in spirit" probably refers to a poverty which is voluntarily chosen, those who are led by the Spirit to identify with the poor and the humble in the world. The opposite is the spirit of pride, the struggle after social and economic upward mobility.

✓ **Blessed are those who mourn, for they shall be comforted.** Blessed and mourn are like happy and sad; they don't seem to go together. Yet most of us have already discovered in life that inner healing comes with tears. The light that shows us our sin heals us.

Again, there is a tendency to spiritualize this beatitude. Some say it refers to those who mourn for their sins. Mourning for one's sins is certainly a good example of the kind of mourning which can lead to healing and personal growth. However, there is no need to limit this beatitude in that way. In fact, in my own life I rarely have any kind of abiding growth or happiness that has not come at the cost of some tears.

" **Blessed are the meek, for they shall inherit the earth.** (See Psalm 37:11.) There are two alternatives to being assertive and aggressive. One alternative is to be a doormat, to let anyone and everyone walk all over you, to completely repress your own wants and desires for another. In that direction lies sickness.

The other alternative is to be like the river reeds which stand straight, yet have enough flexibility to bend down to the ground before a fierce wind. When the hurricane passes, huge trees are shattered, but reeds spring back up as sprightly as before. We are not talking timidity, we are talking inner poise.

✓ **Blessed are those who hunger and thirst after righteousness, for they shall be satisfied.** One meaning of hungering after righteousness is desiring that justice be done. *The Jerusalem Bible* translates this, "those who hunger and thirst for what is right." It is a profound dissatisfaction when children starve because of the economic policies of wealthy companies, when powerful leaders push nations to the brink of terror, when the poor have their liberty taken from them. It is the ardent desire of kingdom citizens for the blessings of earth to fall not just to them, but to all persons equally. It describes those who cannot easily accept life's goodies until all God's children have access to the goodies.

There is an inner dimension to this beatitude as well. The world's ills have their roots in our hearts. So we face the profound yearning to be whole, to be full of love, to be more than we are. It prompts us to ask what hungers operate within us? What desires command our time and attention? Be careful about that for which you hunger and thirst. You might get it. One's spiritual discoveries will never exceed one's spiritual hungers. If you are satisfied with a low-level relationship with God, that's probably all you will ever know.

Blessed are the merciful, for they shall obtain mercy. I saw a bumper sticker that said, "I don't get mad; I get even." But getting even never brings the satisfaction one thinks it is going to.

Being merciful also extends beyond forgiveness or refusing to carry grudges. Ignatius Loyola once said, "Let it be presupposed that every good Christian is to be more ready to save his neighbor's idea than to condemn it." It is funny how we are so much quicker to respect our neighbor or our neighbor's property than our neighbor's ideas. Even when we don't condemn them, we feel an obligation to correct them.

Blessed are the pure in heart, for they shall see God. As an adolescent, I thought that purity of heart meant that one was free from sexual fantasies. Now some folks say that these fantasies are essential to psychological health. I don't think that I believe that, but I am convinced that I had the wrong interpretation of this beatitude. Purity of heart is more accurately defined as sincerity, transparency of intention and character, and purity of purpose. Kierkegaard simply said, "Purity of heart is to will one thing."

Blessed are the peacemakers, for they shall be called sons of God. Notice that the makers of peace, not the peaceful, are called God's children. In situations in which I am involved, are people more sensitive and loving because of me? Or do I cause tension?

Blessed are those who are persecuted for righteousness sake, for theirs is the kingdom of heaven. John Wesley once said that the best helps to growth in grace are the ill-usage, the affronts, and the losses which befall us.

After looking at all eight Beatitudes, we need to ask ourselves what in the world this is all about. There is no way that these qualities describe happiness or success by any definition. It is not the poor, the sad, the meek, the dissatisfied, the soft, the naive, the meddlers, or the odd balls of society who know happiness. What is going on?

One difficulty is that we read the Beatitudes as if they were commandments. They are not. No one is commanded to be anything in this section of scripture.

Second, no matter how high or deep one pushes the meaning of blessed, the Beatitudes are not promises any more than they are commandments. Jesus is not offering rewards; he is stating facts.

Jesus seems to say that it is wimps who get blessed. Yet we despise wimps; no one wants to be one. And perhaps there is a clue to interpretation. We prefer to get our religious stimulation from the suave, the successful, and the sophisticated. But the Bible directs our attention to society's rejects—the kind of folks, in fact, with whom Jesus spent much of his time.

If one is financially secure, happy, self-confident, successful, and sophisticated, one does not need an additional blessing. The Beatitudes were not commandments, and if they don't describe you, you don't need to feel guilty. But you may feel as if you just missed Christmas.

Discussion and Action

For Beginning

Share with each other the paraphrases you wrote in preparation. Compare your list of persons who demonstrate the eight qualities.

For Discussion

1. Compare the description of kingdom citizens offered in the Beatitudes with 1 Corinthians 13 and with the description of the fruit of the Spirit in Galatians 5:22, 24.

2. Which beatitudes best describe your current spiritual state? Which indicate your greatest need for growth? Which is least clear to you?

3. In what ways does discipleship to Christ call for a person to be a wimp? In what ways does it not?

4

Discipleship
Matthew 5:13-15

Preparation

In Session Two we talked about the effect the Sermon on the Mount has on you, whether it discourages or energizes you. This session discusses the effect your own faith has on others. Observe carefully your life during the week. When are persons most aware of your faith? Why? How does it make them feel?

Understanding

Oliver Wendell Holmes said, "I might have entered the ministry if clergymen I knew had not looked and acted so much like undertakers." Apart from his unfairness to undertakers, what does this say about the attractiveness of discipleship? Jesus said, "Let your light so shine that folks will see your life style and be drawn to God."

The little section of the Sermon on the Mount which this session examines tells of the relationship between the disciple and the world. But before we look at that it might be well to ask, "To whom is the Sermon addressed?"

The Sermon on the Mount, according to most scholars, is not really one unique sermon but a collection of the sayings of Jesus from throughout his ministry and assembled by Matthew to represent the style of Jesus. If this is so, then the Sermon is more than a one-shot message. It is a major emphasis of much of the preaching of Jesus through his whole life.

Whether it is an anthology of the sayings of Jesus or one sermon, Matthew presents it as one sermon that is addressed to a particular audience.

"Seeing the crowds Jesus went up on the mountain . . . and his disciples came to him" (Matt. 5:1). Both crowds and disciples are mentioned. What picture comes to your mind? Did Jesus depart from the crowds to give private instructions to the Twelve? Or do you see Jesus surrounded by the Twelve and just a bit further out a crowd of, say, several hundred listening in? Is the Sermon addressed to the Twelve or to the crowd?

Matthew 7:28 shows that the crowds were listening. But it is still not clear whether the Sermon was for them or for the Disciples. Other major addresses in Matthew's Gospel were addressed to the Twelve.

It may seem that it doesn't matter much who was the audience. But some argue that the Sermon was addressed only to the twelve Disciples, and, therefore, it represents a particular high calling within the normal Christian faith. This sets up two different grades of Christians. That is, anyone can be a Christian, but certain Christians are called to live a higher way, with a little extra dedication not expected of ordinary Christians.

On the other hand, if the crowds were the audience, then Jesus is describing qualities he expects of everyone called into the kingdom. He is talking about the way of God for all people.

By the same token, when Jesus tells his audience they are salt and light, who does he mean? Is everyone within the sound of the voice of Jesus salt and light? Or is it just the ones called to what we neatly name "set-apart ministries"?

As usual, I would like to have it both ways. The presence of the crowds is important to show us that this is not just a special call for spiritual giants. The Sermon on the Mount is the will of God for all people. On the other hand, the presence of the twelve Disciples is important to help us remember that the kingdom-life described in the Sermon on the Mount is a Christ-centered life. It comes out of the response to the call of Jesus to join the new community. One simply cannot live the Christian ethic without the Christian experience. *Disciple* is not a word for a special kind of Christian. It means all of us who have heard in Christ a call to follow.

When one unites intimately with Christ, then the Sermon on the Mount becomes a description of the journey. It is the life from God which becomes in us "salt of the earth." It is the light which Jesus kindles which is the "light of the world."

This session deals with only four verses of the Sermon on the Mount (5:13–16). But they are an essential link between the Beatitudes and the rest of the Sermon. The Beatitudes sketch a certain quality of life, a certain character. That character also reflects the nature of God. One could go over the Beatitudes and read them as a description of God. God is meek; God is merciful; God is a peacemaker; God identifies with the poor.

The verses in this session also declare that this same quality of life is essential for the health of the world. It is salt. It is light.

Salt has so many uses that sermons on "You are the salt of the earth" can go most any direction. We use salt mainly for flavor. The ancient world thought of it more as a preservative. Eberhard Arnold, remembering that saline solutions are used in injections, talks of it as a life-giving element. A paleobiologist thinking of the "primordial stew" of the oceans could speak of salt as the place of the origin of life. None of these meanings would be entirely wrong. The essence of salt is that it is not an end in itself; its purpose is to bring wholeness to something else.

Light has the same quality. It is true, as verse 15 points out, that no one lights the lamp and hides it. But it is also true that no one lights the lamp and looks at it. One uses the lamp in order to see something else.

The focus of this paragraph is not on the glory of the disciple, but on what the disciple can do for the world. This is congruent with the message of the Beatitudes. The goal of the Christian faith is not to create Christians. The goal of the Christian faith is to create the kingdom—a society—a new world. Individual Christians find fulfillment as they become part of that purpose.

There are two basic ways a disciple relates to the world. Either the disciple can conform to the values of society, or withdraw from society to live a different style of life in cultural isolation, like the Amish or the Orthodox Jews. This scripture points to a third way. A disciple is called to live by a radically different set of values—as described in the Beatitudes—but to live this kingdom-life in the midst of the world. "It does no good," Jesus said, "to light the lamp and hide it under a bushel."

Notice where the command lies in these verses. Disciples are not commanded to be salt; they simply are. Also, they are not asked to produce their own light. The command describes where this ought to take place, in the midst of the world.

As we become open to the kind of women and men described in the Beatitudes, the world will be seasoned and illuminated. Out of the spirit of poverty, meekness, and love, in the midst of purity, peacemaking, and suffering the kingdom will be wrought.

"Let your light shine in the midst of the world so that they may see your good works and give glory to God." It is not that one becomes meek, or that one loves in order that one might get a good reputation. It is not even that the world might be salted or illuminated. Love which is generated to change a situation is not love. Rather, one simply lives in kingdom ways. If we see results from living that way, well and good. But if not, it is still the way we are called to live.

That means if I love someone and they do not change, I have not failed. If I am meek before someone and they do not soften, it was not in vain. If I am merciful to someone and they are not merciful in return, my mercy is not wasted. If there has to be some special purpose for our action, the purpose is not focused on results or on ourselves, but on faithfulness or on an action offered in response to God.

Discussion and Action

For Discussion

1. Would you expect a higher standard of Christian living from a Catholic or a Quaker? A fundamentalist or a liberal? A preacher or a lay person? Why?

2. What would you like to see happen in your congregation that would make it more inviting to unchurched people?

3. Some Christians wear a small cross or other symbol of their faith. Some use bumper stickers to proclaim their beliefs. Is this a good idea? What is your reaction? What do you feel is the reaction of non-Christians to this practice?

4. What do you see as signs of distinctiveness in your group? Signs that it is "salty" and "alight"?

5. Have there been times when you would rather not be identified as a Christian?

6. Discuss the last two paragraphs.

5

Challenge to Conventional Wisdom
Matthew 5:21-48

Preparation

Carefully read the scripture, making notes of passages which are special challenges to you.

Understanding

Normally the place where a sermon was given is not important. In this case, the place is highly symbolic. Matthew calls attention to the mountain because he is drawing a deliberate comparison between Jesus giving the Sermon on the Mount and Moses receiving the commandments on Mount Sinai.

There is a trick in that kind of deliberate comparison, however. It goes awry easily. On the one hand, some interpreters use the comparison to make Moses look bad. They continue to harp on how inadequate the Old Testament law was and how superior the New Testament message is. In doing this, they make too sharp a distinction between what God said in Jesus and what God said through the Old Testament.

The fact is, Jesus did not go in a completely different direction from the teaching of the Old Testament. What he taught lay along the same trajectory as the best of the Old Testament.

On the other hand, other interpreters use the comparison to emphasize the smooth flow between Moses and Jesus. They say Jesus is a new Moses. They point out that nearly every line of the Sermon on the Mount can be paralleled in the Old Testament. In doing this, they make too little of the uniqueness of Jesus as a special act of God's revelation.

The fact is, Jesus did announce a new era in God's dealings with people. Jesus carried within himself a unique transparency to

God and so was given the title "Son of God" (Phil. 2:9). There was a freshness and an authority in the message of Jesus which was not a repeat of the message of Moses.

In this chapter we will not set the teaching of Jesus in opposition to the law of Moses, or to the Old Testament teaching, or to the Jews of Jesus' day. There is no particular gain in finding out that Jews of Jesus' day needed the message of Jesus. When we interpret in this manner, we become like the person who said, "I hope that George and Helen hear the preacher's sermon on judging today because they sure need it."

It will be far more fruitful to contrast the teaching of Jesus in the Sermon on the Mount with our human nature or with conventional wisdom of our day.

In Matthew 5:21-48 Jesus gives his interpretation of the law, the Torah. This was a standard practice of rabbis. It did not mean that the law was being criticized or abolished, as Jesus was careful to point out in 5:17-19. It meant that the inner meaning of the law was being explored. The phrase "But I say to you . . . " is translated in *Texts in Transit* as "My position is . . . ." Another translation might be "My interpretation of the meaning of this law is . . . ."

The six examples in this section of the Sermon on the Mount probably illustrate the way Jesus interpreted all of the Old Testament. But these six areas are of great importance to the citizens of the kingdom.

The first example (5:21-26) is about conflict resolution. It is also an expansion on "Blessed are the peacemakers." Making peace is not simply refraining from war or the killing of others. It is a way of life in which one strives to handle all anger and inner violence honestly and openly in order to avoid destructive outbursts and damaging insults. The fabric of human interaction is easily destroyed. Respect for others means that I will not permit my anger to have free rein.

Jesus makes two suggestions for establishing and maintaining shalom in the kingdom. First, he suggests that we give reconciliation priority over worship. Second, he suggests that we do not hesitate but take the initiative to establish reconciliation without delay. The kingdom of heaven is a network of human relationships in which reconciliation has top priority.

The second example of the inner meaning of the law (5:27-30) has to do with human sexuality. Often we read this section as a message about personal purity. That is only part of the issue. A deeper issue has to do with sexuality and marriage, the concern for the well-being of one's marriage partner. Sound marriage harmony is based on more than sexual fidelity. Inner loyalties of the heart are equally important. In the kingdom of heaven, covenants between persons are honored.

The third example (5:31–32), maybe a sub-point of the second, deals with divorce. Again, our tendency is to read these with only an eye to avoiding personal sin. This is not the only concern here. In the strongly patriarchal society of both the Old Testament and New Testament world, the position of women needed special protection. The "certificate of divorce" was a step toward protecting the rights of women. Jesus takes that protection one step further by pointing out that any divorce jeopardized the rights of the woman. Citizens of the kingdom of heaven have special obligation to guarantee the rights of persons who are at a disadvantage socially, as well as an obligation to honor commitments.

The next area (5:33–37) is honesty. When a court or civil agency requires an oath, it is seeking to do the same thing Jesus is doing in this example. It is seeking to promote truthfulness. However, it seeks to do this by putting life into two compartments, one under oath and the other not under oath. Under oath a person will tell the truth or else face the penalties. Not under oath a person will tell the truth unless it is inconvenient.

The assumption behind the words of Jesus is that one should not compartmentalize life and to attempt to do so is destructive. Truth cannot be imposed upon liars with the use of an oath. Truth flows from the inner integrity of one who has entered discipleship. Integrity and sincerity are essential characteristics of the messianic community. Jesus asks us to be clear and simple in our speech. There are no occasions when dishonesty is appropriate.

The fifth example is retaliation, how one deals with antagonism (5:38–42). The Old Testament law of retaliation quoted by Jesus restricted vengeance and prevented excessive violence in the community. Jesus, penetrating to the heart of that law, spells out its intent in even clearer terms. The aim is reconciliation. Work for redemption rather than simply limiting revenge.

The notion of getting even is so deeply ingrained in us that we feel the world is unfair when bullies do not get punished. Most legal systems are based on an exact punishment meted out to those who do wrong. Can Jesus have really meant for us to neglect punishment? This is such a novel idea that Jesus used four examples to hammer it home, one from interpersonal life, one from legal life, one from political life, and one from economic life.

The last of the six interpretations (5:43–48) speaks of loyalty. The second half of the saying, "hate your enemy," does not come from the Old Testament. It apparently was a proverb, a common addition to the first half, "love your neighbor." The theme of this popular addition to the Torah was loyalty. We are loyal to "our guys" and hate those who are enemies of "our guys."

Jesus denies this proverb and expands on the Torah by declaring that all people fall into the category of "neighbor," that is, one to be loved. The command to "love" your enemies does not mean to feel nice toward them. It means to do something good for them, to reduce hostilities.

With the use of several examples Jesus undermines any concept of loyalty which would place some people outside the category of folks to whom I owe concern and love. Denominational loyalty and national pride alike have a demonic side when we realize what it can do to our relationships to those not of our own denominations or nation. Boundaries between people and groups of people are counterproductive to the kingdom of heaven.

Discussion and Action

For Beginning
Of the six areas dealt with in this session, in which do you feel yourself still bound by conventional wisdom? In which do you feel yourself living in the freedom of Jesus' new insight? What about your study group? Your congregation?

For Discussion
1. Recall instances from your own experience when you have given priority to reconciliation over worship. Are there times when you have not?

2. Cite examples of the statement with which the writer closes: "Boundaries between people and groups of people are counterproductive to the kingdom of heaven." Are there exceptions?

6

Testing Our Motives
Matthew 6:1-18

Preparation

Go over the Lord's Prayer thoroughly this week. Which phrases are made more clear by other parts of the Sermon on the Mount?

Understanding

All the counsels about the quality of life in the new kingdom can be followed for the wrong reasons. One can walk the second mile, pluck out the infected eye, work for reconciliation, or bless one's enemies for the wrong reasons. Matthew 6:1 is translated this way in the *Cotton Patch* translation, "See to it that your effort to do right is not based on a desire to be popular. If it is, you'll get no help from your spiritual Father."

Agnes Day and Gloria Mundey serve on the same worship committee, but they do not see eye to eye. Agnes is a Jesus person. She wants to sing scripture songs, to read from *The Living Bible*, and to say "Thank you, Jesus" a half-dozen times in each paragraph. Gloria, on the other hand, insists that worship ought to be done with good taste. The music should be Bach, the scripture RSV, and the language of worship formal.

What makes the problem so devastating, however, is not the difference in their opinion, but the way in which they choose to quarrel about it. "Gloria," sniffs Agnes, "isn't really worshipping. She just wants to show off her education. 'The Old Rugged Cross' was perfectly good enough for her before she went to college."

Gloria, on the other hand, explains to everyone who will listen that Agnes feels socially inferior, has a husband who abuses her, and has children who are a disappointment. "Religion, for her, is an escape from reality. She doesn't want faith; she just wants an emotional high."

Freud, Marx, and Nietzsche are not normally heroes to spirituality. Yet we need to hear their message. Paul Ricoer called them the "masters of the school of suspicion." He pointed out that one of their greatest contributions was that they taught us to be suspicious of our motives.

Freud pointed out that hidden beneath motives which we are more easily aware of are motivations which are often unconscious and which have something to do with our psycho-sexual development. Marx showed that unaware we most often do things which are to our political and economic advantage. Nietzsche examined the way in which we protect middle-class morality and power. These thinkers were not so much skeptics about faith. They were just suspicious of the motives of persons who believe. What motivates folks to believe what they do? What are they *really* saying?

We need to listen to them. We can see it easily enough in other folks. The self-deception of the Nazi Christians who supported the persecution of the Jews is clear enough for us to see. It takes no special keenness on our part to see that when the Afrikaner of South Africa makes a religious case for apartheid, it is not really piety but politics which is the motivation.

But we frequently use the insights of these "masters of the school of suspicion" as weapons directed at others. It is often easier than examining the real issues at stake. Agnes Day and Gloria Mundey, and a host of their brothers and sisters in the church, are quite interested in other people's motives. But are we as quick to notice the prominence of various self-serving motives in our own piety?

What happens when our prayers, our giving, even our fasting become instruments for flouting the purposes of God? Prayer concerns for many people today are items of personal concern: a new car, a better job, the braces on the kid's teeth. Very seldom does one hear a prayer saying "I'd like to grow in holiness."

The special concern lifted up in 6:1–18 is the ease with which the purity of our motives in the spiritual life is contaminated with pride and the desire for recognition. Other contaminants could just as easily be mentioned. Freud said we might catch ourselves practicing piety in order to please a human father or as a way of denying and repressing our sexual drives. Marx said some practice their religion as a way of protecting economic interests. Nietzsche said that our religion often reflects our struggles for power or the protection of the status quo.

We might deny that any of these contaminants operate in our own spiritual life. In fact, Freud predicted that we would deny it, but that it would be dangerous to deny it. The truth is that purity of motives is very elusive. A lifetime is too short to get one's motives sorted out so that they are free from ego-drives.

Stewardship, devotions, and spiritual discipline are mentioned by Jesus as examples of piety especially prone to ulterior motives. The first of these is the practice of giving. Most Bible translations speak of alms, which is a word we do not use. Substitute tithing, stewardship, giving to disaster relief, the food pantry, you name it.

It takes a powerful motivating force to part us from money. The Christian church has not been ashamed to use public opinion as one of those forces. One wonders, especially, about the practice of soliciting memorial gifts. Or, to use another example, there is more than one congregation which is somewhat at the mercy of one or two big contributors. And occasionally one meets one of those contributors who is willing to throw a little weight around. The phrase "sound no trumpet before you" (RSV), like "blowing your own horn," may be picturesque exaggeration, but we know exactly what it refers to.

The other side of the coin, of course, is persons who give gifts in utter secrecy but for their own satisfaction. Over-concern about motives leads some people to give less and less. Some have used verse 3 to justify their resistance to pledges or to offering envelopes.

Prayer is another practice vulnerable to errors in motive. It seems particularly tragic when prayer, that opening of one's self before God, becomes a tool to accomplish something else entirely.

It is bad enough that our prayers (particularly those led by the pastor on a typical Sunday morning but also our own in private devotions) become routine and stereotyped. But we can deal with that. Everyone's prayer life will have times of dryness and spiritual silence.

But when one no longer expects any sense of communication in prayer, it is a short step to the place where prayer becomes an act not directed at God at all, but at others.

Perhaps it is because we have not learned the lesson about oaths that we are faced with the dilemma about prayer. In the passage on oaths we heard Jesus pressing us for transparency, openness, and honesty in our relationships within the church. Because we have not practiced that enough, the church is the last place we would want to admit our sins or our times of spiritual dryness. And not being honest about ourselves leads us, in our devotional lives and in our worship, to pretend that nothing at all is wrong with us.

Notice that Jesus intends for us to keep on praying, fasting, and giving alms. It is not the practice of these which he speaks against. He is demanding that we continue to examine our own motives within the practice.

One's motives are not the same as one's feelings. When one does not feel like praying, the best thing to do is to pray until one does feel like praying. If you don't feel like singing on Sunday morning, pick up the hymnal and sing as lustily as you can until you do feel like it. The principle at work here is that my faith and my desire to praise and pray is not dependent on my fickle feelings. Deep within I want, with all my heart, to live in the presence of God. The fact that I don't feel like it from time to time is irrelevant. Just be perfectly honest with yourself and with any who ask about what you are doing.

The final arena open to unworthy motives is fasting. I have found that fasting privately does not have as much impact on my life as fasting corporately. When I covenant with three or four others to fast, a different spiritual dynamic is at work. How does this square with the passage we are currently studying?

Jesus and his disciples were accused of never fasting. This must have meant that they lived what Jesus preached. Although they fasted, the surrounding society was not aware of it. No gloomy faces there.

Discussion and Action

For Discussion

1. In Matthew 6:14 Jesus picked one phrase out of the Lord's Prayer for special emphasis. Why did he choose that one?

2. How can we determine whether our motives in our own spiritual journey are self-serving or Christ-like?

3. Is it wrong to experience gratification in giving? What is the basis for your answer?

4. How does the teaching of Jesus in this passage speak to your prayer experience?

5. How has fasting been a helpful part of your spiritual journey?

6. Conclude your session by focusing on the *Cotton Patch* translation of Matthew 6:1 quoted above.

7

Trusting in God
Matthew 6:19-34

Preparation

Reflect on the things in your life which make you "anxious."
Make a list of them. Is there any pattern in the list? Reflect on what
would need to happen to convince you not to worry about
these things.

Understanding

Nowhere in the Sermon on the Mount is the challenge of
Jesus to conventional wisdom any sharper than in 6:19-34. Yet
these passages about money and trust need to be interpreted
carefully.

The problem is how literally to take the words of Jesus. The
thought of Jesus can be betrayed by taking these words too sim-
plistically, too literally, and too irresponsibly. The message is more
frequently betrayed by applying it only to "spiritual" matters or by
taking the words as an ideal which is not practical for our world.
We dare not reduce the challenge for disciples to be as "harmless
as doves" on the one hand or the challenge for them to be as "wise
as serpents" on the other.

Too many people have read the Sermon on the Mount and
come away believing that money was evil. And, since money was
evil, bankers and brokers were slightly tainted. In fact, everyone
who made money was slightly evil, and those who made more
money were more evil.

Even if we won't admit it, money and property consume a
large portion of our interest. In church, one can get an argument
more quickly over our government's financial policies, socialized
medicine, or farm supports than one can over the nature of the
atonement.

Since we tend to think that money is evil, we avoid examining its use in the light of the gospel. Unexamined attitudes are usually unredeemed attitudes, and they sneak out and betray us at times. With our tongues we confess that money isn't everything; we live simply and trust God. Yet our heated discussions, our unwillingness to criticize economic systems that are destructive of society, and our sharp eye for good bargains betray us.

We do not live without money. And, furthermore, there are many places in the Gospels in which Jesus counsels sound investments, wise spending, thrift, and financial responsibility. Therefore, we need to face the question of the place of money and property in the kingdom of heaven.

Economics is in this part of the Sermon on the Mount because property is one thing which most frequently limits our spirituality; it blocks our trust in God.

Jesus is not advising financial irresponsibility but the sorting of priorities. Anxiety is caused by honoring systems mutually exclusive with the values we hold. And one of the systems mutually exclusive with the attitudes, relationships, and values described in the Sermon on the Mount is the system of greed and conspicuous consumption that marks our society. Mammon is simply the Aramaic word for affluence.

Living in the most affluent country in the world seems to lock even the most spiritually sensitive into a lifelong battle with Mammon. How can we live in our world and yet maintain the values of the Sermon on the Mount?

One clue to the dilemma is found in the last two verses. We need to start there and move backward through the chapter. "Seek first God's righteousness and the kingdom" and "be not anxious."

We have defined the kingdom as the authority, the dignity, or the reigning of God in establishing human networks which reflect shalom. It is God-centered but it is established in a human context. Throughout the Sermon on the Mount we have seen values of that kingdom lifted up: reconciliation, loyalty to covenant, protection of rights, mercy, peacemaking, integrity. The word *righteousness* is another term from the same bin. It refers to the establishment of right relationships, of justice and peace on earth.

Seeking first the kingdom means that our economic practice and our property use needs to be regulated by these same concerns. Trusting God is not simply a matter of waiting with folded hands until God drops a check into our laps. It is trusting that our budgets, our investment practices, our use of property, and the manner in which we earn our money *all* ought to submit to the values of the kingdom. And if there appears to be a conflict between sound investment practices and kingdom values, we refuse to put protection of property or economic gain over kingdom values. We will continue to work to reconcile the sound investment with kingdom values precisely because we trust those values first.

A farmer once went to the fair to engage a hired hand. He asked the first man he came to about his qualifications and the man replied, "I can sleep on a windy night."

"Well!" thought the farmer. "I'd much rather have a man who can work than one who can sleep." So he left the young man and looked elsewhere.

But, alas, there was none other available that day so at evening he returned to the first young man and hired him.

Five or six weeks went by with no particular trouble. The farmer and his new hired hand got along well. Then, in the seventh week, a terrific windstorm sprang up in the middle of the night. The farmer, fearing that gates would be banging, roofs torn loose, or live stock scattered, sprang from his bed and raced to waken the hired hand.

He shook him and called him, but the young man would not awaken. "You certainly can sleep on a windy night!" shouted the farmer in disgust as he left him in bed and dashed on to protect the farm alone.

But once the farmer was outside, an amazing thing greeted his eyes. No gates were swinging in the wind because all the gates were securely fastened. No roofs were rattling; all were nailed down tight. No shutters were swinging. The tarps on the machinery were lashed secure. The livestock was safe. Nothing was blowing about the yard because everything had been picked up.

Now the farmer knew what the hired hand meant when he said that he could sleep on a windy night.

The hired hand knew that if he sought to do his work well as he went along, then he did not need to be anxious on a windy night. Disciples know that if they put first the kingdom—that shalom network of human and divine relationships and attitudes—they will not need to be anxious about anything else.

Discussion and Action

For Beginning

Three times in Matthew 6:25-34 Jesus said, "Do not be anxious." He also gave seven reasons why we should not be anxious. Pick out each reason and state it in your own words.

For Discussion

1. Discuss the writer's comment that persons living in our affluent society are locked into a lifelong battle with Mammon. Is the struggle worse for affluent nations or for underdeveloped nations?

2. How important is the "profit motive" to American life? Does the Sermon on the Mount contradict the profit motive or regulate it?

3. Share in your study group any stories of persons receiving an unexpected gift just when it was needed. Does the passage about the birds of the air suggest that one can always count on such unexpected gifts?

For Action

Invite someone from a Third World country to speak to the group on this passage of scripture as they see it. Suggest that they contrast the attitudes toward money in America with that of their home country. What are the similarities? In what particular ways does this scripture speak to the different situations in different ways?

8

Judge Not
Matthew 7:1-7

Preparation

Can you recall some personality trait, childhood dream, or budding talent of yours which was squelched by criticism? What would it take to recover that dream?

Understanding

Living in the kingdom community has its hazards. One is excessive zeal. Such zeal manifests itself in a quickness to spot other people's sins. Matthew 7:1-7 is necessary instruction for living in the new community.

"Judge not, that you be not judged." Sometimes these words are taken to mean that what your brother or sister does is none of your business. Two factors make this an attractive interpretation. The first is that our society places heavy emphasis on individualism. There are all kinds of social pressures against meddling in another person's affairs.

A second factor is that few of us have had experience living in the kind of society that the Sermon on the Mount portrays. Our congregations fall short of being the kingdom. Often our Bible study groups are more intentional attempts at discipleship and kingdom relationships, but even there we have only rare models for the kind of community which cares enough to hold its members accountable without getting heavy-handed or maudlin.

If we interpret this passage to mean that the conduct of our sister or brother is no concern of ours, we miss the last part of verse 5 as well as a host of other New Testament passages (Matt. 18:15; Luke 17:3; Gal. 6:1-2). These passages insist that disciples have obligations to one another. It is a part of the responsibility of the community of disciples to help each other discern good from evil.

Paul calls it bearing one another's burdens and says it is the "law of Christ."

The manner in which we exercise this spiritual responsibility for one another, says Jesus, is critical. And it is probably at this point that the new community stands its greatest test in our time. How we deal with our weaknesses is a delicate matter. It can be redemptive or destructive to the community.

In our highly competitive society, even conversation can have winners and losers. We talk about whose kid was the first to walk, who can quote the most sports statistics, why my interpretation of scripture is better than yours, and how much louder laughter I can get for my jokes than yours. Normal patterns of conversation place one person in a "one-up" position and the other in a "one-down" position.

I've seen persons so skilled at competitive conversation that they gain enough points to be one-up without saying a word. One raised eyebrow is devastating when properly timed.

Peter was an impetuous and rash sort of disciple. He was always rushing into things with his foot in his mouth. In the language of transactional analysis, the "child" in Peter was active and free. It is worth noting that after three years of intimate association with Jesus, Peter never lost this spontaneity. Jesus was not a put-down person. Even while Peter was in training to be a disciple, Jesus never squelched the child in him.

Judgment squelches. Judgment takes inappropriate power in a relationship and leaves one person in a one-down situation. Judgment is taking on ourselves a task which ultimately belongs to God. It is as if we cannot entirely trust God with the business.

Our judgments rebound on ourselves (7:2). It is a widespread human trait to be alert to faults in others while we are blind to the same or related faults in ourselves. It is known as projection; we project onto others the problems we are fighting within ourselves. The truth is that folks "give themselves away" more by the nature of their criticisms than any other act or word. "But what will the neighbors say?" is not asked by folks who never talk about their neighbors.

One step toward spiritual mutual responsibility that avoids judgment is "first take the log out of your own eye." Jesus asks us to be alert to the tendency to projection and to first look within. The catch is that we cannot see logs in our own eyes, let alone take them out. Discovering logs in our eyes requires that we submit ourselves to the counsel of trusted disciples. We should consider ourselves fortunate when we are shown that a log is there. Even better is we should admit that it is there. And it's nearly marvelous if we should actively solicit others to help us in log-removal.

Those who wish to give spiritual direction are warned that they should not attempt it unless they are themselves in spiritual direction. Those who would be counselors are encouraged to undergo counseling themselves. I cannot hear you speaking helpfully to my anger until I know that you know what anger is. I will resist hearing your advice about my lust or greed until I know that you understand the depth of your own. I can receive your sympathy over the loss of my parent when I know that you have lost your own.

On the other hand, is it good to have no sense of judgment at all? Is it not necessary to be discerning about things? In order to probe this question, let us use the word judgment for an individual's evaluation of another person. Judgment is my opinion about another's action, attitude, or ideas.

Discernment is a community process; it is the community's search for truth. Judgment is spotting that the brother or sister has a speck in one eye. Discernment is sitting down with the brothers and sisters and asking, "What could we all do in order to see better?"

The verse about pearls before pigs (7:6) describes the need for discernment. Moral discernment is a necessity for kingdom citizens. And the church is called to speak out prophetically when it has a word of moral discernment. Jason Martin in *The Sermon on the Mount* has this to say:

> I do not want my church to be tongue-tied about the following issues:
> - anything that devalues and degrades human personality,
> - the estimated 1.5 million abortions performed annually in the United States,
> - tax structures that strap the poor but shelter the rich,
> - rampant militarism.
>
> Nor do I want my congregation to be passive about conditions within the church such as judgmentalism, moral laxity, avoidance of resolving conflict, phony spirituality, false prophets, and the excesses of the electronic church.

Discussion and Action

For Beginning
You have just received a letter asking for your recommendation of a person applying for a job. You are asked to be candid about that person's abilities, character, and personal qualifications. Your answer will be kept secret. How does this scripture affect your answer?

For Discussion

1. You are a district-level executive in your denomination, working with a congregational search committee. You have a pastor in mind for the congregation, but it is a person who got into moral difficulties in a previous congregation. You are confident that the pastor is repentant and will not fall again and you want to offer a second chance without prejudice. How much do you tell the search committee?

2. Not many congregational leaders sit down in council to discern what should be their church's response to current moral issues. Should we?

3. How influential are the decisions made at the national level in the small group's decisions about right and wrong?

4. Can the group think of examples of "competitive conversation?"

For Action

As a group reflect on the degree of your congregation's spoken or unspoken judgment of persons. Decide on actions which can increase acceptance within the congregation without lessening standards.

9

Way of Life; Way of Death
Matthew 7:13-23

Preparation

From histories, or from older people in your congregation, gather some stories of occasions when your church may have disciplined its members.

Understanding

Teachings about false prophets make me uneasy. We rarely preach or hear sermons on false prophets because it goes against the toleration we strive to maintain as Christians. In fact, this whole section seems to run counter to the previous session on not judging.

Most of the few sermons or articles I have seen about "false prophets" are from ultra-conservative groups who describe false prophets as people who teach and believe as we do. To be fair, I have also known "our side" to take passages about false prophets and use them to describe the folks who condemn the folks like us!

Seeing how the teachings about "false prophets" can easily become a weapon with which to clobber people one doesn't agree with and to make us leery lest we violate Jesus' teaching about judging, many ignore these words about false prophets altogether.

If there is truth in Christianity's claims, however, then it is possible to take that truth and subtly bend it until it is no longer true. In former times the Christian Church made a distinction between "orthodox teachings," "unorthodox teachings," and "heresy." Orthodox meant correct. Unorthodox meant teachings that weren't perfectly in line with the official teachings of the faith—a little screwy, perhaps, but still within the boundaries.

Heresy described those teachings which were so far wrong that they undercut or otherwise denied the truth of the faith.

All kinds of problems arise. One is that somebody has to draw the lines. How far can truth be stretched and still be orthodox? How wild can unorthodoxy be before it becomes heresy? Who draws the lines?

Another problem is that truth always needs to be examined, explored, and taken to its limits. Education depends on the freedom to inquire into new ideas. Labeling the false prophets ahead of time robs that inquiry of integrity.

Another problem is that after some of the historic battles over heretical ideas have cooled down for a few centuries, we have looked back and discovered that there was, indeed, considerable truth in what we once labeled heresy.

Despite the problems, there is still danger from heresy and it is important to learn to identify the false. This section of the Sermon on the Mount touches that issue.

In much of the Sermon on the Mount we are warned about ourselves. In Matthew 7:13-23, it seems, we are warned about others. Three classes of false prophets may easily seduce the Christian community from kingdom ways.

First is the warning about the easy road. Other people seem to have it easier than Christians. In fact, some branches of the Christian church seem to preach an easier way of life than the one described in the Sermon on the Mount. Positive thinking, successful Christian living, four steps to salvation, and a host of others make it seem that the Sermon on the Mount must surely be too strict.

Second is the warning about wolves with sheepskins. These are deceptive persons who sabotage kingdom ways from within. They may talk kingdom language but the effect of their lives is to undermine the way. "It's too radical. Jesus was speaking in an exaggerated style to attract attention; he never expected one to take it seriously. It's a beautiful ideal. It would be nice if everybody followed it, but since they don't we have to be practical."

The third is a warning about those who smother the kingdom message with religion. Being religious, even being outstanding in preaching, healing, spectacular wonder-working, or evangelism is not the way to the kingdom. The most frequent abuse of the faith is to limit it to what are narrowly called "spiritual" matters.

These warning passages point us in two important directions. The first grows most directly out of the text. In my description above, I have put words into the mouths of the "false prophets." But in 7:13-23, Jesus does not identify any particular ideas that the false prophets taught which made them false. Instead, Jesus points to their fruit, their life. This shifts the ground from orthodoxy, correct doctrine, to orthopraxis, correct practice.

Back when denominations were more strict about the standards of membership or standards for clergy, some denominations held heresy trials. If one was convicted of heresy, of believing something which the church taught to be false, then one lost membership or ordination in the denomination. Other denominations tested for correctness of doctrine in a different manner. Instead, members of the church hierarchy tested one's life. A person could be suspended from membership or a pastor could lose ordination for behavior which was inappropriate to a Christian. It was a test of orthopraxy.

The verdict we have passed on ourselves is that we abused this practice. We suspended folks from membership over minor items such as wearing neckties or hats, but not for pride, gluttony, avarice, or sloth. But while we may have focused on the wrong sins, something in the idea was right. As this section of the Sermon on the Mount shows, the manner of our life is a test of our faith.

What manner of life, then, is "orthopractice"? Much of the Sermon on the Mount begins by naming a deed—such as killing, prayer, divorce, fasting—and then discussing the attitudes which lie behind the deed. So perhaps the "fruits" about which Jesus talks in 7:16-20 are not so much deeds, but attitudes. Even a "desire to serve the underprivileged" can be a way to bolster one's own ego.

This brings us to the second direction of the text. Perhaps the "false prophets" against whom we most need to guard are within us. The temptations would have no power were it not our own hearts urging us to look for an easier road, a more spectacular way, religious comfort rather than confrontation. We seek what "works for me" rather than "what is edifying to the church." The Sermon on the Mount leads one on a journey within. The narrow gate (7:14) is hard to find because it requires first that we lay down our lives, our defenses, our striving, and even our piety. The way is narrow because it leads through the valley of the shadow of the death of ourselves.

The Beatitudes describe the soft spot in God's heart. One gets to know God through that spot. The Sermon on the Mount describes the qualities of life and the qualities of the society that are God's realm. One who lays self aside and follows there, knows the kingdom.

Discussion and Action

For Discussion

1. How do you understand the writer's warning about those who smother the kingdom message with religion?

2. Which reveals more about a "prophet"—what he says or how he lives?

3. How can we recognize and guard against "false prophets" within ourselves? How can your study group help?

4. Discuss the conflict between identifying false prophets and not judging. How are these two reconciled?

10

Hear and Do or Hear and Not Do
Matthew 7:24-29

Preparation

Read through the Sermon on the Mount again. Make a special note of those parts of the Sermon that have challenged you to make a change in your attitudes or life style. What has been your decision about that challenge?

Understanding

Some decisions can be put off forever. If someone asks you whether you agree with the new theories about subatomic particles, you might be able to dodge making a decision for a long time and not be any the worse for it.

Other decisions are in the nature of "forced choices." You are confronted with a decision you cannot avoid. If you are asked to come and help wash dishes, you cannot avoid the decision. You either help, or the dishes get washed without your help.

The Sermon on the Mount strikes one with the power of a forced choice. One needs to decide what to do with it. It is not an interesting lesson to be discussed. It is not a decision that can be fudged with a "yes-and-no" answer. If the decision is delayed, one will find that the unconscious decisions of everyday life have moved us in the opposite direction. And that undermines the foundations.

Sometimes the history of scholarship on the Sermon on the Mount seems to be a history of excuses. All sorts of people have been apt at figuring out reasons why one need not really follow the Sermon on the Mount. In our discussion throughout this unit we may have been guilty of diluting the demands. But the Sermon plants a seed of permanent dissatisfaction in our souls. We cannot leave it alone.

Bonhoeffer said, "Humanly speaking, we could understand and interpret the Sermon on the Mount in a thousand different ways. Jesus knows only one possibility: simple surrender and obedience, not interpreting it or applying it, but doing and obeying."

The closing of the Sermon on the Mount makes it quite clear that Jesus does not intend for his words to be simply a high ideal which we all admire. He expected his words to be done. "Whoever hears these words of mine and *does* them . . . ."

The beginning of the message of Jesus was "Repent." His call to repentance demanded a complete revolution of inner and outer life. He wanted to remove the obstacles of personal and social wrong which keep the individual away from God's kingdom. In the Sermon on the Mount, Jesus spells out the characteristics of repentance.

We know, and can talk at great lengths, about the meek, the merciful, the poor, and the peacemakers. But what does it look like when, as a group, we covenant together to live this way? What would happen to our congregations if members would seriously consider what shape the church is to take in accordance with the Sermon on the Mount?

In describirg the Beatitudes, our third lesson said that they were not commandments. Throughout the rest of the Sermon on the Mount we continue to meet conditions which are impossible to demand of others and which no one could have courage to lay upon himself. The action of the kingdom of heaven penetrates the world like light and salt in free, spontaneous working.

The effort to be perfectly transparent and open in our relationships (Matt. 5:33-37), the effort to be loyal to our covenants in thought and emotion as well as action (Matt. 5:27-30), or the effort to regulate our financial affairs by trust, justice, and love (Matt. 6:19-43) all are futile. We cannot command this effort of ourselves or of others. It is, instead, the result of an unconditional love which controls our lives completely. It is the result of a heart that loves with God's love, an ethic that is life-centered and free, and the indwelling Spirit.

It might be pardonable to add to Jesus' words that if one hears the words of the Sermon on the Mount and tries to do them on one's own steam alone, then that person's situation may be as bad as the one who hears the word and does not do it.

Consider two cases. The first person says, "The words of the Sermon on the Mount are unrealistic. I do not need to obey them." That person then builds a house on the foundation of the conventional wisdom of our society instead. A second person says grimly, "I must follow the words of the Sermon on the Mount. I have to do it." And that person begins building a house on the foundation of obligation. Both houses will ultimately fall. But after the fall of the houses, it may be that the situation of the first person will be better than the second. The first person may be led to see that the wisdom of the "unrealistic" Sermon on the Mount was more realistic in the long run than the conventional wisdom of the world.

The second person, however, is doomed to deeper despair. "I tried to follow Jesus and failed. So I tried harder and failed again."

Following the Sermon on the Mount takes the utmost resolve, the strongest spiritual discipline and inner firmness. Therefore, the springs of its energies must flow from waters deeper than emotionalism or self-improvement.

Jesus did not call disciples and turn them loose. He called them "to be with him." Discipleship was an experience in a small group, an apprenticeship with the master, a model of kingdom living.

A strong case needs to be made for shifting our understanding of the Sermon on the Mount. Heretofore, I have understood it as a demand laid upon me as an individual. Should no one else in the world choose to follow these demands, yet I will follow. Hereafter this, we shall understand the Sermon on the Mount, not as a demand upon an individual, but as a description of a society. It describes the establishment of the State of God which will stand in the sharpest opposition to the State of Mammon. It describes the network of shalom relationships, a network of human relationships with God at its center. Seeing a glimpse of that network, that state, that "kingdom" causes me to long to enter it with such intensity that I will lay down my life for it.

It is like a miner trapped in a cave-in, breathing foul and compressed air which grows more poisonous by the moment. Some rescuer from the outside manages to break a small gap to allow the free and fresh air to rush in. The miner suddenly is given a new lease on life. The body, lethargic from oxygen starvation, suddenly experiences a rush of new energies. The miner is, for a moment, united with the other world which he longs for. And with new resolve, the miner will work for dear life to join the real world.

The Sermon on the Mount does not command, it beckons. In it Jesus uses the phrase "kingdom of heaven" to describe the ideal, the hope. He says, "Here is what the kingdom looks like. Come and join it." But make no mistake, the kingdom is a confrontation with conventional wisdom. It is a confrontation with human nature. It is a subverter of human order. It is repentance, conversion, and radical discipleship. But it is the only breath of fresh air this world knows.

Discussion and Action

For Discussion

1. Should new converts to the faith be taught the Sermon on the Mount? Might it scare them away?

2. How have your views of the Sermon on the Mount changed over the course of this study?

3. The setting of the Sermon on the Mount is studded with references to the authority of Jesus. Where do you accept Jesus' authority for your living? Where do you have trouble accepting that authority? What changes would you like to make?